TEN STEPS
to improve your child's
SCIENCE
for ages 7–8

GW00502905

Let's learn at home

AUTHOR   Peter Riley

ILLUSTRATORS   Maggie Downer / Fred Pipes

Teeth and food

In this step you will find out about your teeth and make some discoveries about your food.

There are four types of teeth. You use them in different ways.

Look at the picture and find the different types of teeth.

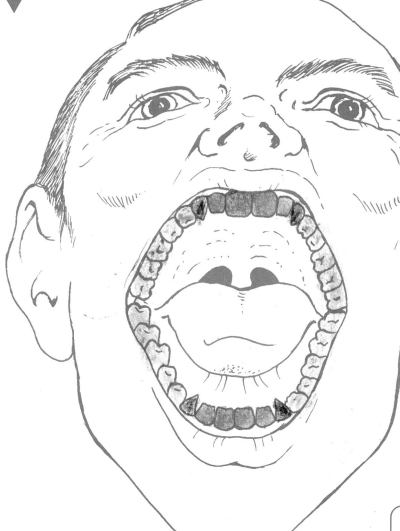

incisors – blue

canines – red

premolars – yellow

molars – green

Now colour in the teeth in these colours.

Count the teeth ▶ in the picture and fill in this table.

Look in a mirror at your teeth. How many of each kind have you got?

Type of tooth	Number in picture	Number in my mouth
incisor	8	8
canine	4	8
premolar	8	4
molar	12	12

Match the teeth to their jobs.

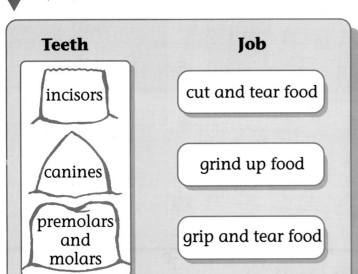

Teeth	Job
incisors	cut and tear food
canines	grind up food
premolars and molars	grip and tear food

An elephant's tusks are incisor teeth.

Do you know how these foods affect your teeth? Colour in red the foods that will make your teeth bad if you eat too many of them.
Colour in green the foods that help keep teeth clean.
Colour in blue the foods that help keep teeth strong.

MILK

Can you remember when your last tooth fell out? What kind do you think it was?

Now turn over

Look at the words on the right. Can you find them in the wordsearch? Colour in each food you find. ▼

c	b	e	e	f	p	y	t	z	m	l	n	a
a	m	u	s	h	r	o	o	m	b	v	o	i
u	q	l	k	i	a	d	m	s	a	c	o	h
l	d	s	g	y	w	t	a	t	f	u	d	n
i	g	p	e	a	n	u	t	x	p	s	l	l
f	z	a	g	p	h	u	o	t	z	t	e	u
l	d	g	h	p	m	n	v	w	r	a	x	s
o	c	h	c	l	q	a	b	x	a	r	z	t
w	d	e	q	e	g	g	w	n	d	d	s	f
e	t	t	l	f	h	j	k	u	i	o	x	p
r	k	t	d	c	m	s	a	u	s	a	g	e
z	r	i	c	e	b	g	h	i	h	h	r	m

cauliflower
beef
mushroom
prawn
tomato
spaghetti
peanut
apple
egg
rice
radish
sausage
custard
noodle

Look at this ▶ trolley full of food.

Meat, peas and beans are foods that help you grow. Colour them in red.

Fruit and vegetables are foods that keep you healthy. Colour them in green.

Butter
Beefburgers
Biscuits
Rice
Baked Beans
cereal
Peas
Pasta
Pasta

These foods give ▶
you energy.
Find them in the
shopping trolley
and colour them
in yellow.

Write down
three foods **you**
eat that help
you grow.
▼

1 __cereal__

2 __Rice__

3 __bread__

Write three foods that keep
you healthy.
▼

1 __fruit__

2 __vegatable__

3 __meat__

Write three foods that give
you energy.
▼

1 __Paster__

2 __bread__

3 __Ricecter__

You may grow
about 6cms
between your
7th and 8th
birthdays.

Great!

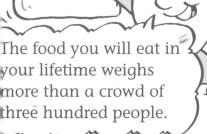

The food you will eat in
your lifetime weighs
more than a crowd of
three hundred people.

Dear Parent or Carer

This step allows your child to identify the four types of
adult teeth and discover that he or she probably does
not yet possess them all. Discuss the last visit your child
made to the dentist and talk about how teeth can be
kept clean and healthy. The fact that different foods
have different functions is introduced but may be
extended by talking about protein in meat, and vitamins
and minerals being essential to keep healthy. Growth
rates vary widely. The example given here is to help your
child visualise how much growth can occur in a year.
Answers on page 30.

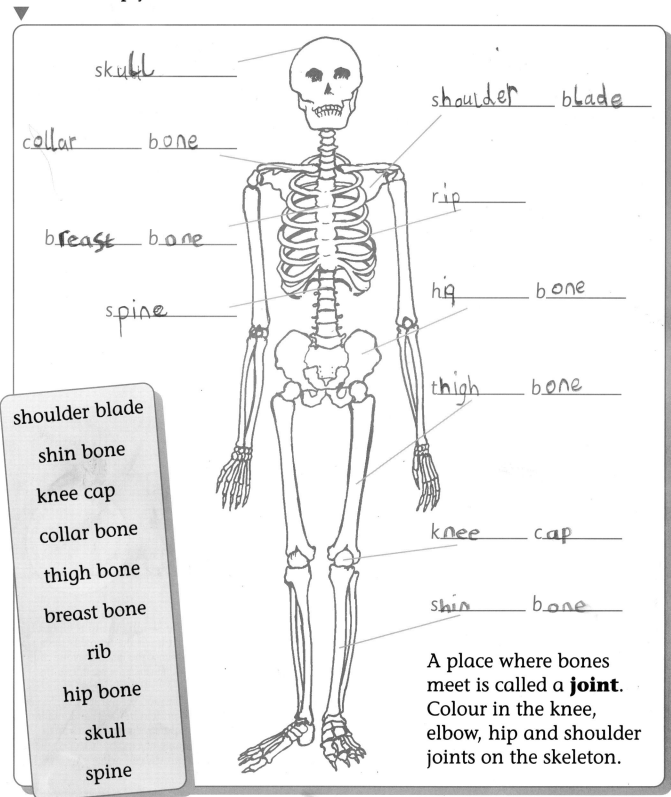

Skeleton and muscles

In this step you will find out about your bones and how your muscles move them.

Write down the names of these bones in the correct spaces. Use the list below to help you.

▼

skull

shoulder blade

collar bone

rip

breast bone

spine

hip bone

thigh bone

knee cap

shin bone

shoulder blade

shin bone

knee cap

collar bone

thigh bone

breast bone

rib

hip bone

skull

spine

A place where bones meet is called a **joint**. Colour in the knee, elbow, hip and shoulder joints on the skeleton.

6

To feel your bones move, ▶ hold your hands as shown. Now turn your right palm over. Feel one bone move over the other.

These bones are called the ulna and the radius. Can you find them on the skeleton opposite?

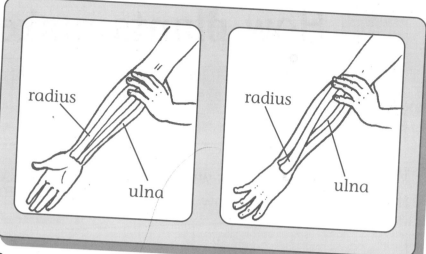

How do the muscles change?

▼

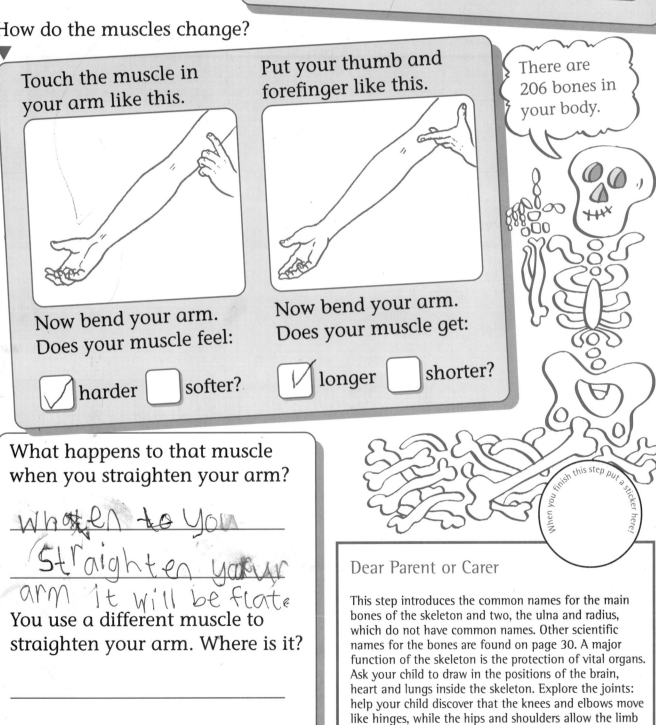

Touch the muscle in your arm like this.

Now bend your arm. Does your muscle feel:

☑ harder ☐ softer?

Put your thumb and forefinger like this.

Now bend your arm. Does your muscle get:

☑ longer ☐ shorter?

There are 206 bones in your body.

When you finish this step put a sticker here!

What happens to that muscle when you straighten your arm?

What en to you Straighten your arm it will be flate

You use a different muscle to straighten your arm. Where is it?

_____

_____

Dear Parent or Carer

This step introduces the common names for the main bones of the skeleton and two, the ulna and radius, which do not have common names. Other scientific names for the bones are found on page 30. A major function of the skeleton is the protection of vital organs. Ask your child to draw in the positions of the brain, heart and lungs inside the skeleton. Explore the joints: help your child discover that the knees and elbows move like hinges, while the hips and shoulders allow the limb bones to move in different directions. Answers on page 30.

How plants make food

In this step you will discover how some of the food that plants make is food for you as well.

Which of these plants will make the most food and grow best? ▼

healthy   unhealthy

Plants that are given fertiliser

Plants that are watered

Plants kept in the dark

Plants that are not given fertiliser

Plants that are kept dry

Plants kept in the light

Draw a healthy plant or an unhealthy plant in each of the pots to show your answers.

Now write on this ▶ care label what this plant needs to keep healthy.

Colour in the parts of this plant ▶
that make most of the food.

Plants move sugar and water
about inside them in tubes.
You can see these tubes in a
stick of celery. Stand a stick of
celery in some ink. After a few
hours look at it and see how the
ink has gone into the tubes.

Here are the parts of some
plants that we eat. Shade in
those that grow underground.
▼

Apple

Potato

Tomato

Carrot

Radish

Lettuce

When you finish this step put a sticker here!

Dear Parent or Carer

Plants need carbon dioxide to make food. This step
allows your child to identify the other things that plants
need. Show him or her the care labels of house plants or
garden plants and extend the activity by allowing your
child to start and care for a small collection of house
plants. After your child has identified the food-making
part of the plant ask how the plant might use the food.
Cut open the celery for your child so that he or she can
see where the ink has gone inside the stalk. Extend the
section on food plants by allowing your child to grow
some radishes in a plant pot. Answers on pages 30–31.

Temperature and conducting heat

Find out how a thermometer works and how heat 'moves'.

A thermometer is used to measure the hotness or coldness of things.

Look at the thermometer that is in warm water.
Now look at the thermometers that are in cold and hot water, and draw in where you think the liquid will be.

This thermometer is in warm water.

This thermometer is in cold water.

This thermometer is in hot water.

Colour in blue the cold places in this room. Colour the warm places in red.

The coloured liquid in some thermometers is alcohol. The silvery liquid in other thermometers is mercury.

Here is a weather chart for five days.

▼

Mon	Tue	Wed	Thur	Fri

20°C	23°C	24°C	21°C	25°C

Which day was the hottest?

Which day was the coldest?

What was the difference in temperature between Tuesday and Wednesday?

Did it get hotter or colder?

Make a bar graph showing the temperature on each day. The first bar has been done for you.
How did the temperature change throughout the week?

▼

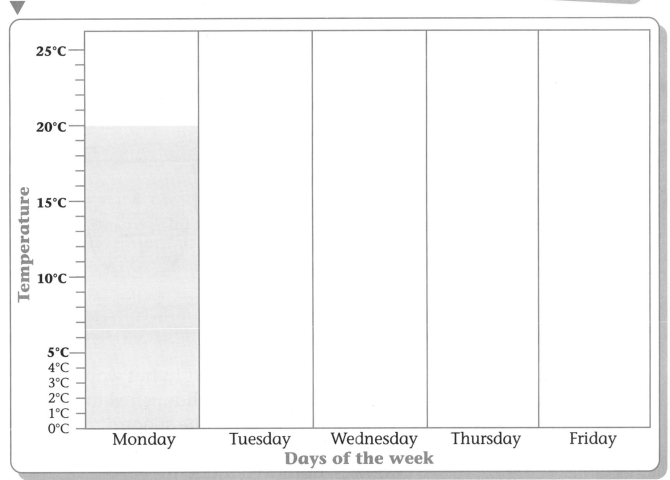

Some materials do not let heat pass through them easily and we can use these to keep us warm. Other materials allow heat to pass through them much more quickly.
Ben needs to dress in clothes that will keep him warm. Which clothes should he wear? Colour them in.

▼

Some animals, such as deer, grow thicker coats in winter to keep them warm.

▲

A metal spoon was left in hot water for a few minutes. What happened to the butter on the end of the spoon?
Draw an arrow on the spoon to show how heat moved along it.

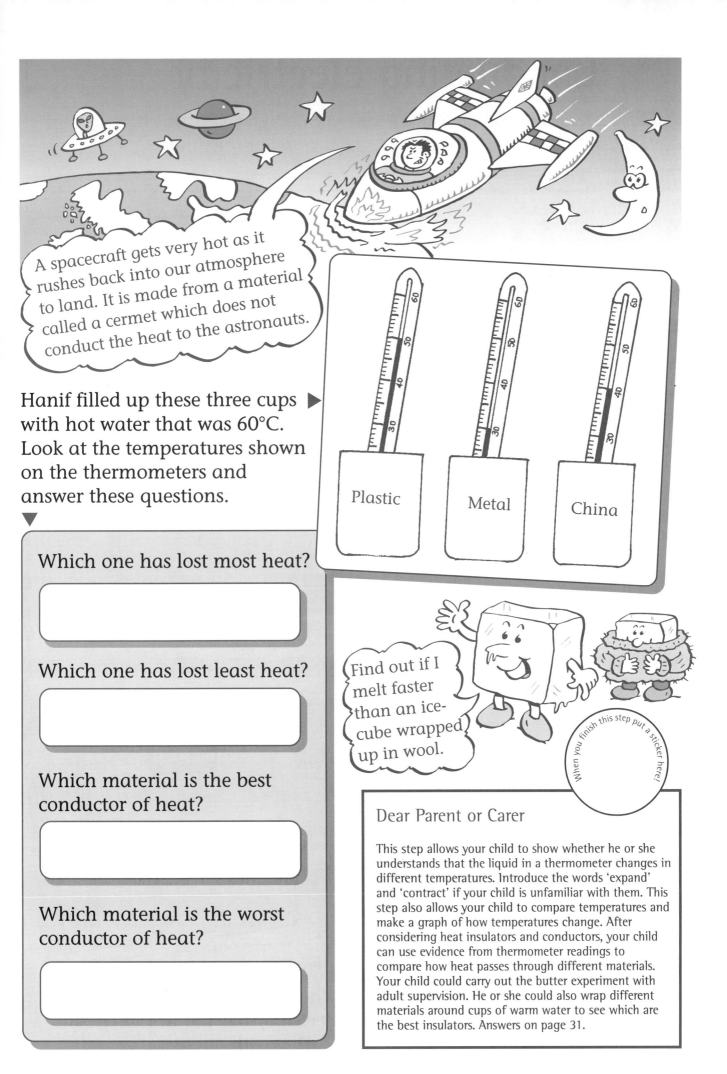

A spacecraft gets very hot as it rushes back into our atmosphere to land. It is made from a material called a cermet which does not conduct the heat to the astronauts.

Hanif filled up these three cups ▶ with hot water that was 60°C. Look at the temperatures shown on the thermometers and answer these questions.

▼

Plastic   Metal   China

Which one has lost most heat?

Which one has lost least heat?

Which material is the best conductor of heat?

Which material is the worst conductor of heat?

Find out if I melt faster than an ice-cube wrapped up in wool.

When you finish this step put a sticker here!

Dear Parent or Carer

This step allows your child to show whether he or she understands that the liquid in a thermometer changes in different temperatures. Introduce the words 'expand' and 'contract' if your child is unfamiliar with them. This step also allows your child to compare temperatures and make a graph of how temperatures change. After considering heat insulators and conductors, your child can use evidence from thermometer readings to compare how heat passes through different materials. Your child could carry out the butter experiment with adult supervision. He or she could also wrap different materials around cups of warm water to see which are the best insulators. Answers on page 31.

Conducting electricity

Electricity flows through a circuit when it is complete. Find out now how to test materials to see if they conduct electricity.

Which switch ▶ allows electricity to flow? Draw it in the gap. Which way does electricity flow? Using the picture, draw arrows next to the wire:

• from the – sign to the bulb;
• from the bulb to the switch;
• across the switch;
• from the switch to the + sign.

Remember: this is a cell.

When cells are joined together they make a battery.

What is stopping the electricity flowing in this circuit? Mark it with a cross.

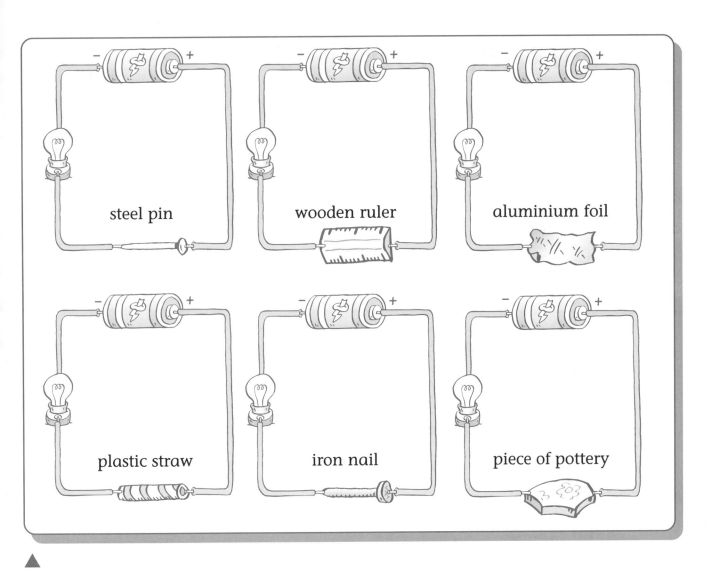

steel pin

wooden ruler

aluminium foil

plastic straw

iron nail

piece of pottery

▲

Do you know which materials conduct electricity?
Colour the bulbs yellow in the circuits that will
allow electricity to flow.

◀ Make a tester like the one shown
in this picture. Use sticky tape to
hold the wires to the bulb and the
cell. Now use it to test different
materials. Which materials make
the bulb light up?

When you finish this step put a sticker here!

Dear Parent or Carer

In this step your child can build up an idea of current
flow and how air and other materials (called insulators)
prevent it moving around a circuit. These ideas can be
confirmed and extended with other materials by helping
your child make a simple tester with a 1.5 volt cell and
a torch bulb and supervising its use. Do not use
rechargeable batteries. Answers on page 31.

Mixing materials

In this step you will discover what happens when you mix some materials.

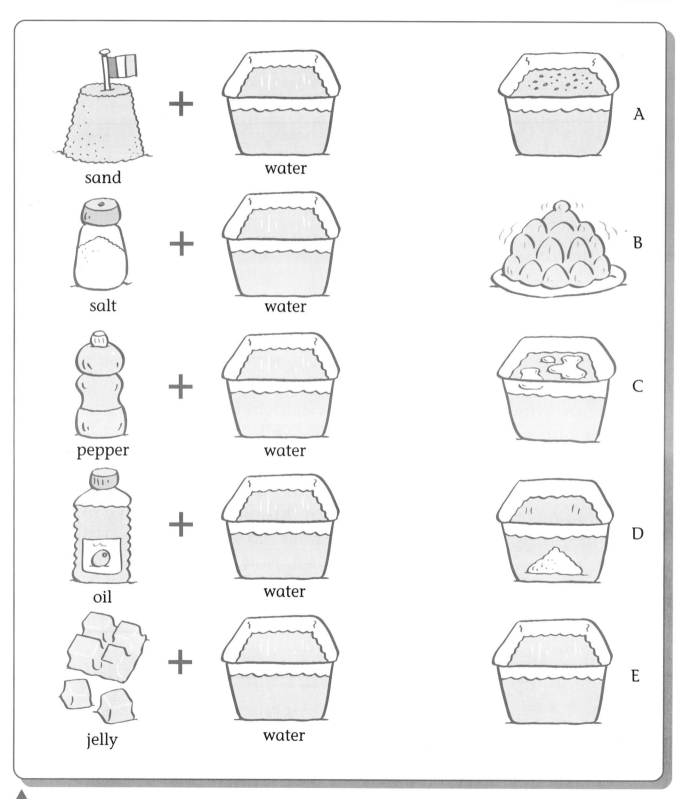

What happens when these materials are mixed? Draw a line from each pair to one of the pictures on the right.

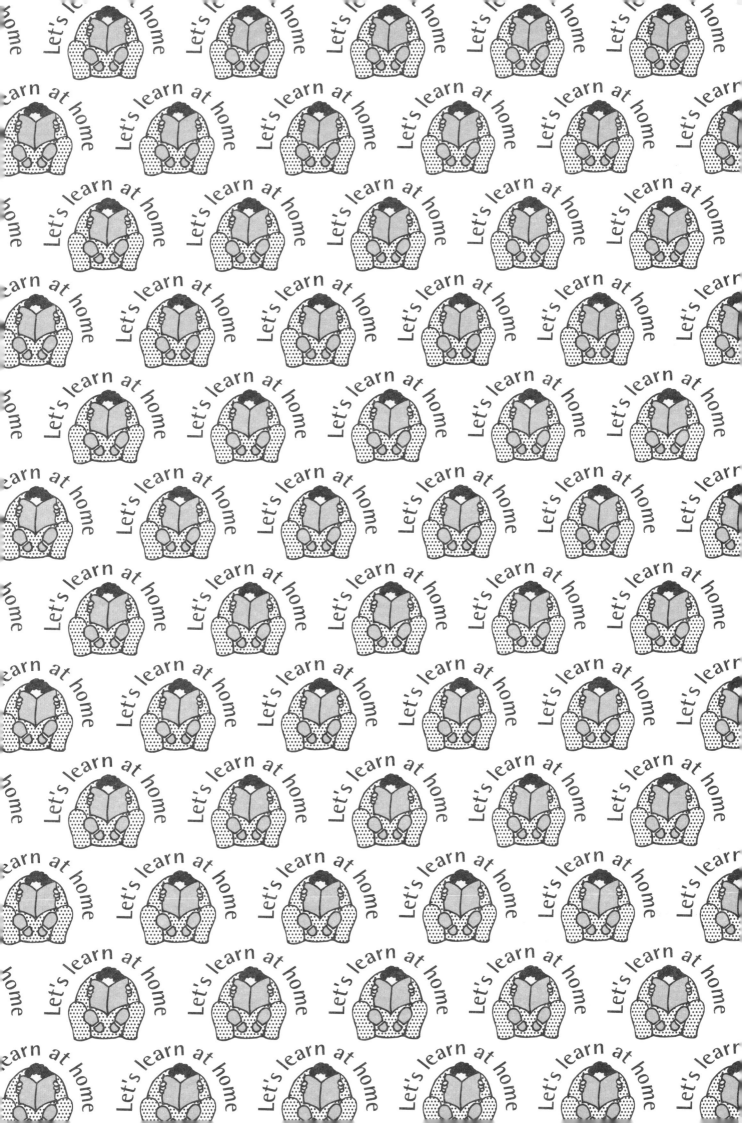

Magnetic Grand Prix

A magnet can pull on magnetic material through cardboard.

You will need fridge magnets, steel paper-clips, rulers, sticky tape, some books and this racetrack to play a Magnetic Grand Prix.

• Put a fridge magnet on the end of the ruler with the magnet facing upwards.

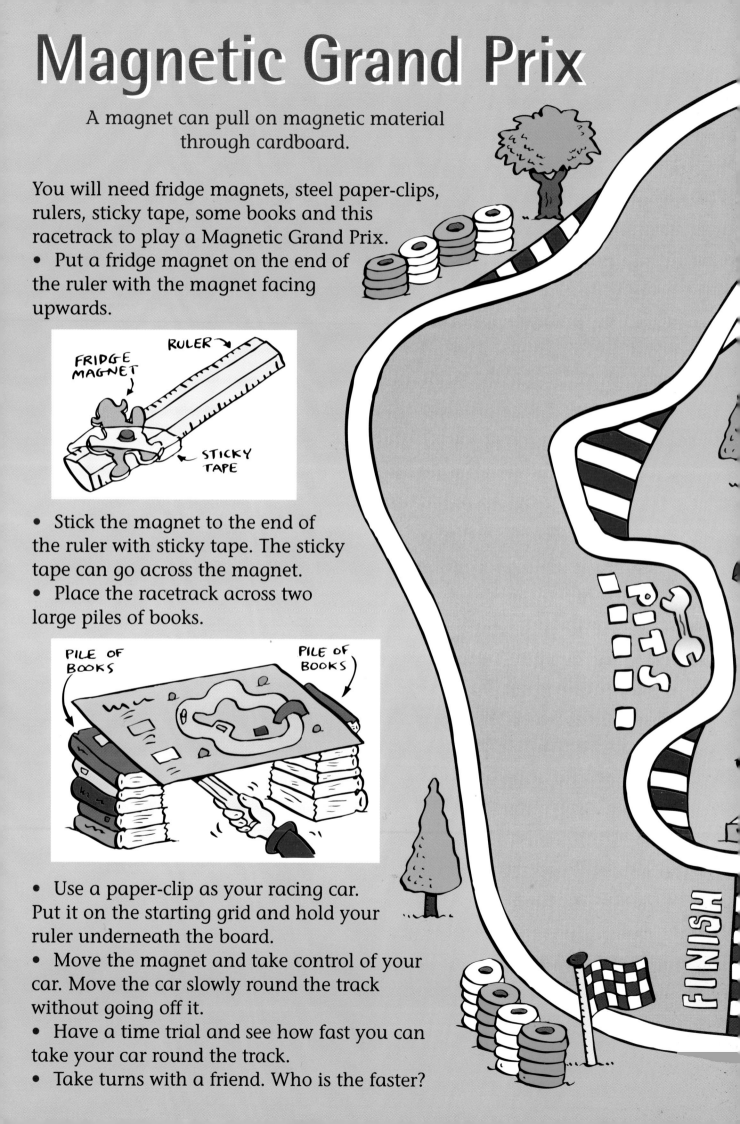

• Stick the magnet to the end of the ruler with sticky tape. The sticky tape can go across the magnet.
• Place the racetrack across two large piles of books.

• Use a paper-clip as your racing car. Put it on the starting grid and hold your ruler underneath the board.
• Move the magnet and take control of your car. Move the car slowly round the track without going off it.
• Have a time trial and see how fast you can take your car round the track.
• Take turns with a friend. Who is the faster?

START

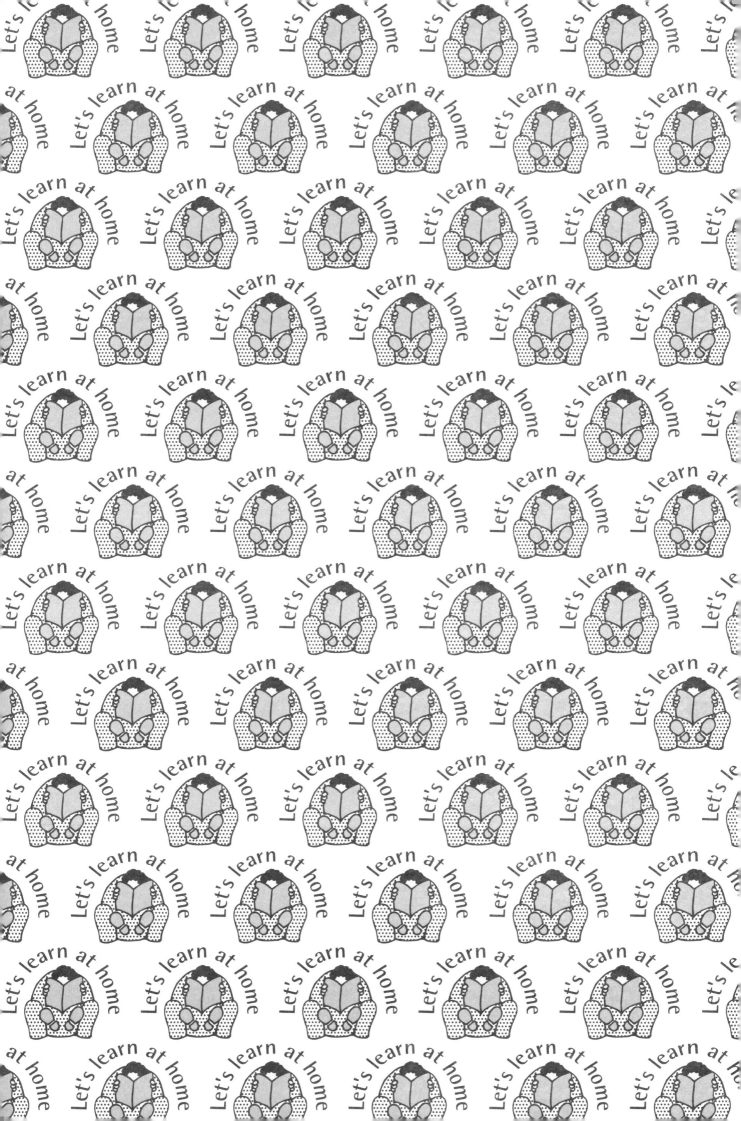

Colour in blue the materials that dissolve in water. ▶

Make some mini-loaves
(You must have a grown-up to help you.)

Dissolve a level teaspoon of sugar in 150ml of warm water.

Add 15g of dried yeast, stir it up and leave until the liquid has a frothy top.

Mix 500g of flour with 30g of margarine and two level teaspoons of salt.

Add the frothy mixture and mix in another 150ml of warm water. Knead the dough, making sure it is not too dry and crumbly or too wet and sticky.

Leave the dough in a warm place until it has doubled in size.

Divide the dough into six batches, then roll each one into a ball.

Put the balls of dough on a greased tray and leave them in a warm place for 15 minutes.

Let a grown-up put them in an oven for 15–20 minutes, and then take them out for you.

Now turn over

j	x	s	u	g	a	r	k
w	m	p	y	e	a	s	t
o	i	l	q	l	r	s	t
o	l	t	s	s	e	y	s
q	k	w	b	a	w	r	s
d	k	n	f	l	o	u	r
e	g	g	u	t	o	p	d

◀ What is in a biscuit? Find eight ingredients in this wordsearch.

Find a cereal box and read what is in it. Write down five of the ingredients. ▶

Stir up some cold cooking oil with water to make a mixture. What happens as you mix them? What happens when you stop stirring?

1.

2.

3.

4.

5.

◀ How many ingredients are mixed together in salad cream? Look on a label and write the number in the box.

Follow these instructions to make a volcano. (Get a grown-up to help you.)

1. Lay down lots of old newspapers. Take the top off an old salt pot.

2. Half fill the pot with baking powder.

Baking powder

3. Build a 'volcano' of Plasticine around the pot.

4. Pour some vinegar into the pot and watch the volcano erupt.

When you finish this step put a sticker here!

The vinegar and baking powder react together. This makes the liquid fizz and flow out of the top of the volcano. The fizzing liquid forms the 'lava' in our volcano. Try again, but this time mix some red food colouring with the vinegar before you pour it in. This will make the lava red when the volcano erupts!

Dear Parent or Carer

This step allows your child to explore the mixing process and see the changes that take place when some materials are mixed. Make sure your child is supervised at all times when making the mini-loaves. His or her measuring skills can also be checked during this exercise. Your child may need help with the word 'ingredients'. Encourage him or her to examine the ingredient lists on a variety of packet foods. Show your child how a little vinegar reacts with a little baking powder to help him or her judge how much of each material to use in making the volcano. Answers on pages 31–32.

Magnets

In this step you can explore how a magnet affects other materials and other magnets.

Which of these ▶ objects will the magnet pick up? Draw lines connecting the magnetic objects to the magnet. Shade in the objects that the magnet will not pick up.

roni

teles

The objects that the magnet does not pick up are made from non-magnetic materials. Their names have got jumbled up too. Write the names out properly.

▼

brbuer

reppa

dowo

tocotn

tcilasp

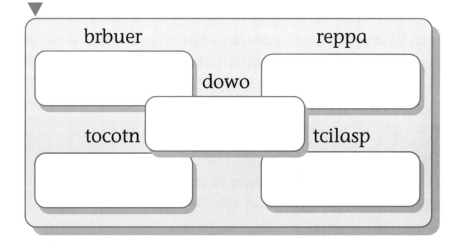

▲

The objects that the magnet picks up are made from magnetic materials. The names of these magnetic materials have got jumbled up. Write the names out properly.

Leon put a piece ▶ of paper over a bar magnet. Then he sprinkled iron filings on the paper. Which pattern did he see?
The pattern shows the lines of force around the magnet.

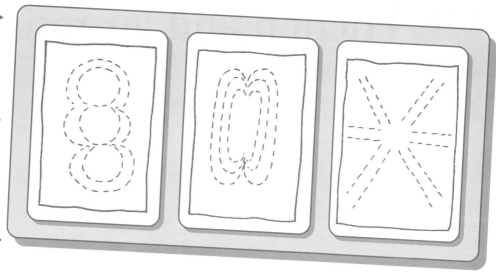

How many sheets of paper will your fridge magnet hold?

▲ Draw arrows on these pairs of magnets to show which way they will move when they are brought close together.

When you finish this step put a sticker here!

Dear Parent or Carer

This step allows your child to identify and explore magnetic and non-magnetic materials. It is a common misconception that all metals are magnetic – they are not. Your child can test more materials using a fridge magnet but make sure he or she does not bring it near television or computer screens, cassette tapes or floppy disks. The pull-out gameboard in the centre of the book allows your child to play a magnetic Grand Prix game. Using a fridge magnet, your child can move a paper-clip around a race track. He or she can then take turns with a friend. Answers on page 32.

Friction and air resistance

In this step you will find out about forces that stop things moving.

Tell someone how friction pulls at your clothes as you get dressed.

Friction is a pushing or a pulling force. It is found where two surfaces meet. Shade in the places in these pictures where there is friction between something and the ground.

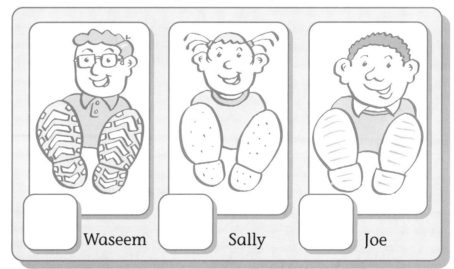

Waseem   Sally   Joe

Who has got the most slippery shoes? Write **S** next to them. Who has got the shoes with the best grip? Write **G** next to them.

Who will win? Draw each car where you think it will stop.

▼

Rub your finger and ▶
thumb together.
Now put a drop of oil
on them and rub again.

Who is reducing friction?
Write **R** next to them.
Who is increasing friction?
Write **I** next to them.

▼

Write down what happens.

_____

_____

_____

_____

When something ▶
moves through
the air it is pushed
on by the air with
a force called air
resistance.

The shape of an
object affects the
way air moves
over it.

Wave your book in
front of you like this.

Now wave it
like this.

1.

2.

What do you feel?

What do you feel?

When did you feel most air being pushed out
of the way of your book?

Some objects are made with streamlined shapes so
that air can flow over them easily. Which objects in
this picture have streamlined shapes? Shade them in.

▼

Mina, John ▶
and Emma opened
their parachutes at
the same time.
Draw and number
them in the order
they will reach the
ground.

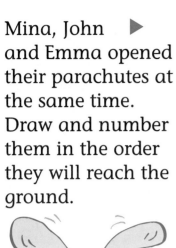

Mina	John	Emma

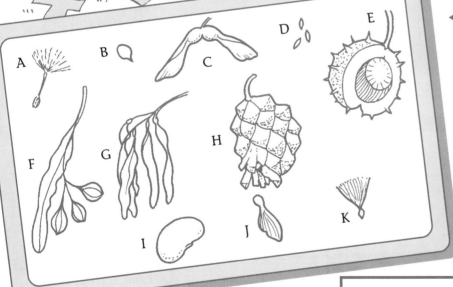

◀ Some seeds use air
resistance to help
them spread out.
Write down the
letters of the seeds
that you think use
air resistance.

When you finish this step put a sticker here!

Write your letters here.

Dear Parent or Carer

This step allows your child to identify where frictional
forces occur, describe their effects and show how
friction is increased and decreased. The car and ramp
activity can be tested by an investigation using toy cars
set up on different floor coverings. Your child may need
help to identify the effect of increasing the pressure on
a surface as increasing the friction, in the activity on
page 23. The work on air resistance may be extended by
making parachutes of different sizes from squares of
cloth or paper, string and a weight such as a toy figure.
Answers on page 32.

Step 9 See-through or not see-through

Find out about how light passes through some materials but not others.

Who can see the light? ▶
Tick the people who can
see the light.

What can you
see through a
drop of water?

B
IGLET
TERSTH
ENSMAL
LERON
ES

Bend a paper-clip
into a tiny circle
and put a drop of
water on it.

What do these words
mean? Draw a line
from each word to the
right meaning.

▼

Ali (glass)

Becky (stone)

David (brick)

Clare (clear plastic)

Alice (water in a glass)

John (wood)

Michael (air)

Lorna (cardboard)

Word	Meaning
transparent	light cannot pass through it
translucent	light passes straight through it
opaque	light is scattered as it passes through it

Which materials in this picture are translucent? Shade them in.

▼

High

Low

▲

If light does not pass through a material a shadow forms on the unlit side. Shade in the shadow of this object when the light is high and low.

When you finish this step put a sticker here!

Dear Parent or Carer

This step enables your child to distinguish between transparent, translucent and opaque materials and to understand the meanings of the words. This step can also be related to studies on the properties of materials. Extend the work on translucent materials by allowing your child to rub some fatty or oily food into newspaper and letting him or her hold it up to the light. Your child may need help in bending a paper-clip to make a small circle in which to put the drop of water. Answers on page 32.

Sound vibrations

In this step you can find out how vibrations make sounds.

Tom is making ▶ a ruler vibrate.

If Tom makes the ruler vibrate more, what do you think will happen to the sound?

▼

Does the ruler:

☐ go up and down?

☐ backwards and forwards?

☐ stay still?

Will the sound:

☐ stay the same?

☐ get louder?

☐ get quieter?

Vibrate your ▶ book or a ruler like this. Which one makes a low pitched sound? Write **L** next to it. Which one makes a high pitched sound? Write **H** next to it.

1.

2.

▲
Which parts of these instruments
vibrate when they are played?
Shade them in.

When you whistle your lips
vibrate and make the air
inside your mouth vibrate to
create the sound.

Fold some paper round a
comb and hum into it.
Make some high and low
pitched sounds. Ask
someone to listen to them.

When you finish this step put a sticker here!

Dear Parent or Carer

This step allows your child to explore the relationship
between vibrations and sounds. While your child may
have little difficulty relating the size of the vibration to
the loudness of the sound, he or she may need help in
understanding the concept of pitch. Words such as
'boom' or 'ping' may be used to illustrate words that we
say have low and high pitches. An elastic band may be
stretched to different lengths between the thumb and
forefinger and vibrated to extend the concept of pitch.
Answers on page 32.

Parents' pages

Step 1 Teeth and food

Page 2: There are eight incisors, four canines, eight premolars (like smaller molars) and twelve molars (including the wisdom teeth) in an adult mouth. A child's first set of teeth (known as the milk teeth) comprises eight incisors, four canines and eight premolars by the age of five. These are gradually replaced starting with the central incisors between the ages of 6–8 and the outer incisors between the ages of 7–9. The first molars appear between 6–7 years of age.

Page 3: The incisors cut and tear food, the canines grip and tear food, and the premolars and molars grind up food.

The sugar in fizzy drinks, sweets and chocolate makes them bad for the teeth; the crunchy, water-laden carrot and celery help to clean them; cheese and milk contain calcium to help keep teeth strong.

Page 4:

c	b	e	e	f	p	y	t	z	m	l	n	a
a	m	u	s	h	r	o	o	m	b	v	o	i
u	q	l	k	i	a	d	m	s	a	c	o	h
l	d	s	g	y	w	t	a	t	f	u	d	n
i	g	p	e	a	n	u	t	x	p	s	l	l
f	z	a	g	p	h	u	o	t	z	t	e	u
l	d	g	h	p	m	n	v	w	r	a	x	s
o	c	h	c	l	q	a	b	x	a	r	z	t
w	d	e	q	e	g	g	w	n	d	d	s	f
e	t	t	l	f	h	j	k	u	i	o	x	p
r	k	t	d	c	m	s	a	u	s	a	g	e
z	r	i	c	e	b	g	h	i	h	h	r	m

Your child may need help grouping beef, chicken and fish as meat.

Page 5: Under foods that help you grow look for answers such as meat, fish, eggs and beans. Under foods that keep you healthy look for answers such as milk, fruit and vegetables. Under foods that give you energy look for bread, cereals and pasta. After your child has completed three foods in each category encourage him or her to think of more examples.

Step 2 Skeleton and muscles

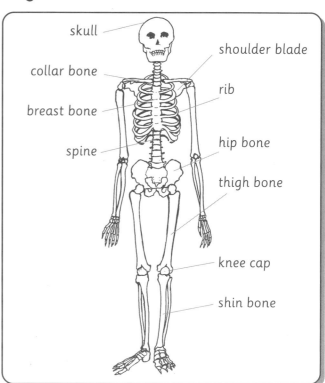

skull
shoulder blade
collar bone
rib
breast bone
spine
hip bone
thigh bone
knee cap
shin bone

Page 6: Point out that a major bone (in the upper arm) has not been labelled and this is called the humerus. Other proper names are: clavicle – collar bone; sternum – breast bone; scapula – shoulder blade; femur – thigh bone; patella – knee cap; tibia – shin bone. Your child may point out that there is a second bone with the tibia. This thinner bone is called the fibula. The spine is also known as the backbone but point out to your child that it is really made up of 26 bones. Each one is a vertebra.

Page 7: Your child can feel how the radius turns over the ulna by placing his or her left hand at different places in the lower arm and turning over the right hand.

The muscle (the biceps) feels harder and becomes shorter.

When the arm is straightened the muscle gets longer and softer. The muscle used to straighten the arm is the triceps muscle which is on the back of the upper arm.

Step 3 How plants make food

Page 8: The healthy plant should be drawn in the pots that are kept in the light, are watered and have added fertiliser. On the care label your child should write that a plant needs light, water and fertiliser to keep healthy. (She or he may also mention that plants often require warmth as well.) By looking at the care labels of plants your child will realise that some plants need more water or light than others.

Page 9: The leaves should be the only part of the plant that is shaded, although green stems also produce a little food.

The celery stalk will need some leaves present. It will take up water faster if it is put in a warm draughty place. The stringy sections which contain the water pipes will have turned blue for a little way up the stalk.

The potato, carrot and radish grow underground.

 ## Step 4 Temperature and conducting heat

Page 10: The level of liquid drawn in the thermometer that is in cold water should be lower than the level in the thermometer in warm water. The level of liquid drawn in the thermometer in hot water should be higher than the level in the thermometer in warm water. Encourage your child to read the scales. The thermometers have the Celsius scale on them.

Your child should shade in blue the shady corner, the fridge and near the ice-cream and the ice drink. The warm places in the room are the window-sill, near the cup of tea and the radiator.

Thermometers should not be put in drinks. Do not let your child use a mercury thermometer and only demonstrate an alcohol thermometer by putting it in cold and warm water.

Page 11: Friday was the hottest day; Monday was the coldest day; the difference in temperature between Tuesday and Wednesday was 1°C; it got hotter. Your child's graph should look like this:

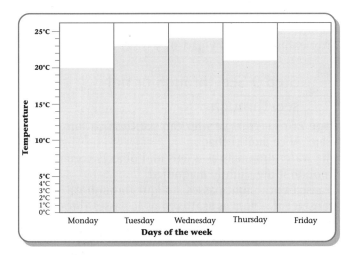

The temperature went up, then down, then up again. The activity can be extended by encouraging your child to read the temperature every day at a certain time and plot it on a graph.

Page 12: To keep warm, Ben would wear the woollen cap, the shirt and sweatshirt, the long trousers, the boots, the lined jacket and the scarf.

The butter melted. The arrow should be drawn from left to right.

Page 13: The thermometer that is in the metal cup has lost most heat; the thermometer in the plastic cup has lost least heat; metal is the best conductor of heat; plastic is the worst conductor of heat.

The unwrapped ice-cube will melt faster than the one wrapped up in wool because the wool insulates the ice from the warm air. It is a common misconception among children that an ice-cube wrapped in wool (or a snowman in an overcoat) will melt faster because the material is making them warm. Their own coats keep their warmth in. However, the wool in this experiment keeps the warmth out, thus keeping the ice cold and slowing down the melting process.

 ## Step 5 Conducting electricity

Page 14: The right-hand switch should be drawn in the gap.

The electric current is carried by electrons which flow from the negative terminal to the positive terminal. (Traditionally, however, current has been represented as flowing from positive to negative.)

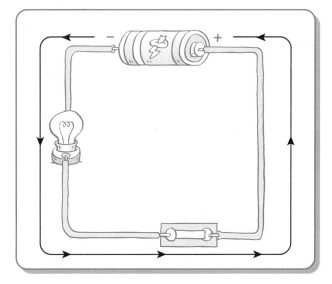

Air is stopping the current flowing so an x should be drawn in the gap in the circuit.

Page 15: Your child should colour in the bulbs in the circuits that have the steel pin, the iron nail and the aluminium foil.

The tester can be made by sticking the wires with sticky tape to the parts of the cell and bulb shown in the picture. Warn your child NEVER to experiment with mains electricity.

 ## Step 6 Mixing materials

Page 16: The mixtures make D, E, A, C and B.

Page 17: The items coloured in should be the bath salts, the coffee granules, the sugar and the soap powder.

Your child must be supervised at all times during this activity. Before baking the mini-loaves, pre-heat the oven to 220°c, Gas Mark 7.

Page 18:

j	x	s	u	g	a	r	k
w	m	p	y	e	a	s	t
o	i	l	q	l	r	s	t
o	l	t	s	s	e	y	s
q	k	w	b	a	w	r	s
d	k	n	f	l	o	u	r
e	g	g	u	t	o	p	d

The ingredients will depend on the cereal. Encourage your child to look for familiar words such as those in the wordsearch, and to spot new words such as wheatgerm and maize.

The oil forms smaller and smaller globules as it is stirred and the mixture becomes whitish. When the stirring is stopped, the oil separates from the water and floats on top of it.

There may be ten ingredients in salad cream. One of them will be a stabiliser used to stop the oil and water separating.

Page 19: The fizzing in this reaction is due to the release of the gas carbon dioxide. You may tell your child that real lava is molten rock and is hot because it comes from deep inside the Earth.

Step 7 Magnets

Page 20: The objects that the magnet is able to pick up are the safety pin, the paper-clip, the nail, the scissors and the pin. The objects shaded in should be the rubber, the piece of wood, the thread, the plastic pen and the paper.

The magnetic materials are iron and steel. (Metals such as aluminium and copper are not picked up by a magnet.)

The non-magnetic materials are rubber, cotton, paper, plastic and wood.

Page 21: Leon saw the middle pattern.

Magnets with opposite poles close together will join together; magnets with the same poles close together will push each other apart.

Magnetism works through non-magnetic material. A fridge magnet may be used to demonstrate this effect by moving a paper-clip around the racetrack in the centre of this book.

Step 8 Friction and air resistance

Page 22: The places where there is friction are: the place where the frog touches the ground; the seat and

shoes of the person sitting down; the shoes of the person and the paws of the dog; the shoes of the person pushing the box and the bottom of the box. Your child may observe that friction pulls on socks and sleeves, shoes and wellington boots.

Sally has the most slippery shoes; Waseem has the shoes with the best grip.

Page 23: The middle car will win followed by the car on the left, and then the car on the right.

The oil reduces the friction.

The people polishing the floor and oiling the bicycle are reducing friction. The person applying the brakes to the bicycle and the person carrying someone on his back are increasing friction by increasing the pressure between the two surfaces in contact – the brake blocks and the wheel rim, and the shoes and the floor.

Page 24: In picture 1 the book pushes air across the face which may also lift the hair. In picture 2 the book does not push air onto the face. The child will feel most air being pushed out of the way when he or she holds the book as shown in picture 1.

The streamlined objects are the modern racing bike, the car, the rocket and the aeroplane.

Page 25: The order of the parachutists is John, Emma and Mina.

The seeds that use air resistance are A, C, F, G, J, K. Air resistance slows down the fall of the seed and increases its chance of being blown well away from the parent plant by the wind. Plants also use animals to disperse their seeds: the animals may disperse the seeds by carrying them on their fur, through their digestive systems, or even by throwing the seeds away after eating the fleshy part of a fruit.

Step 9 See-through or not see-through

Page 26: The people who can see the light are Ali, Clare, Alice and Michael.

The water drop acts as a lens and objects seen through it are slightly magnified.

Transparent – light passes straight through it; translucent – light is scattered as it passes through it; opaque – light cannot pass through it.

Page 27: The translucent materials are: the window in the door; the tracing paper; the greaseproof paper; the cloud; the steam from the kettle; the cover over the fluorescent light and the shower curtain.

When the light is high the shadow is on the opposite side to the light and is short. When the light is low the shadow is on the opposite side to the light and is long.

Step 10 Sound vibrations

Page 28: The ruler goes up and down; it gets louder. The low pitched sound is made by vibrating the book or ruler as shown in picture 2; the high pitched sound is made by vibrating the book or ruler as in picture 1.

Page 29: The drum skin, guitar strings, triangle, violin strings, xylophone blocks and cello strings should be shaded in.